Scriptu
for Ev

OTHER BOOKS IN THE SERIES

Scripture Verses
for Every Day

Amgad Maher Salama

Paulist Press
New York/Mahwah, NJ

The scripture quotations contained herein are from the Authorized or New King James Versions.

Cover design by Sharyn Banks
Book design by Lynn Else

Library of Congress Cataloging-in-Publication Data

Salama, Amgad Maher.
    Scripture verses for every day / Amgad Maher Salama.
        p. cm.
    ISBN 978-0-8091-4500-3
    1. Devotional calendars. I. Title.
    BV4811.S198 2008
    242′.2—dc22

                                                            2007034429

Published by Paulist Press
997 Macarthur Boulevard
Mahwah, New Jersey 07430

www.paulistpress.com

Printed and bound in the
United States of America

Contents

Dedicated to the spiritual growth
of every reader
that in everything God, the Holy Trinity,
may be glorified, blessed, and exalted.

Introduction

This collection of scripture verses for every day of the year is structured around a different theme for each month.

By contemplating the scriptures, it is my hope that you will become more aware of your relationship with God and be drawn closer to the love that God offers each and every human being, no matter what one's color, race, or creed.

For each day of the year, you will find a scripture quote and an accompanying reflection. However, do not be restricted by the current day and the month, for you may find a particular theme that reflects your own journey at any time as a source of inspiration and prayer.

Ultimately, the aim and focus of this book is your relationship with God, so let the Lord guide you in prayer, and listen to your heart as you reflect on the scriptures and make them your prayer for the day.

January

Faith

1

...thou hast known the holy scriptures, which are able to make thee wise unto salvation through faith which is in Christ Jesus. (2 Tim 3:15)

Strengthen our faith so that we may draw near to you and overcome life's challenges.

2

I am not ashamed of the gospel of Christ:...For therein is the righteousness of God revealed from faith to faith.... (Rom 1:16, 17)

The good news invites everyone to approach God in genuine devotion with sure reward.

3

Now the just shall live by faith: but if any man draw back, my soul shall have no pleasure in him. (Heb 10:38)

The Lord is pleased with those who place their trust in him—spiritually, materialistically, and socially.

4

Therefore being justified by faith, we have peace with God...By whom also we have access by faith into this grace wherein we stand, and rejoice in hope of the glory of God. (Rom 5:1, 2)

The effects of faith are peace, comfort, strength, fearing nothing, and hope in the eternal. Strengthen my faith, Oh Lord.

5

...let us run with patience the race that is set before us, looking unto Jesus the author and finisher of our faith.... (Heb 12:1, 2)

Help us to run on track, abiding by your love.

6

I have prayed for you, that your faith should not fail. (Luke 22:32)

Knowing our human vulnerability and importance of faith, how great it is that our Savior himself thus cares to uphold us.

7

For whatsoever is born of God overcometh the world: and this is the victory that overcometh the world, even our faith. (1 John 5:4)

Our firm belief in a loving and merciful Lord leads us not only to avoid sin but to overcome the trials of the world.

8

Your faith should not stand in the wisdom of men, but in the power of God. (1 Cor 2:5)

Christian faith surpasses intellect; it's understood more by the heart and experience.

9

The apostles said unto the Lord, "Increase our faith." (Luke 17:5)

The disciples asked the Lord to broaden their faith, which he did by revealing himself to them. Broaden our faith, Lord, by revealing yourself to us.

10

Examine yourselves, whether ye be in the faith;...
(2 Cor 13:5)

Practicing Christianity is having good thoughts, actions, and words so that people may see Christ through us and glorify our heavenly Father.

11

Rooted and built up in him, and stablished in the faith, as ye have been taught, abounding therein with thanksgiving. (Col 2:7)

Not knowing the full depths of the faith shouldn't lead you to doubts; search the scriptures for answers until you're satisfied.

12

And beside this, giving all diligence, add to your faith virtue;...that ye shall neither be barren nor unfruitful in the knowledge of our Lord Jesus Christ. (2 Pet 1:5, 8)

Living the faith is also daily prayer, repentance, praise, contemplation, obeying the commandments, and increasing in virtues.

13

Who by him do believe in God, that raised him up from the dead, and gave him glory; that your faith and hope might be in God. (1 Pet 1:21)

Our faith is not a contrived philosophy, but is based on a risen Savior, who died for all humans.

14

By grace are ye saved through faith; and that not of yourselves: it is the gift of God. (Eph 2:8)

Fill us with your grace so that we will experience your love and do your holy will.

15

Now faith is the substance of things hoped for, the evidence of things not seen. (Heb 11:1)

Help us to see you more clearly and experience your love more intimately.

16

Having then gifts differing according to the grace that is given to us, whether prophecy, let us prophesy according to the proportion of faith. (Rom 12:6)

The more faith we put in our Shepherd, the greater are the blessings he confers.

17

Watch, stand fast in the faith, be brave, be strong.
(1 Cor 16:13)

Give us strength to live as Christians despite ridicule or persecutions.

18

What doth it profit, my brethren, though a man say he hath faith, and have not works? can faith save him?... Even so faith, if it hath not works, is dead, being alone. (Jas 2:14, 17)

Are we any different from Satan who believes in God's existence but has no salvation? Lord, make our faith visible through our actions.

19

He saith unto them, "Why are ye fearful, O ye of little faith?" Then he arose, and rebuked the winds and the sea; and there was a great calm. (Matt 8:26)

Lord, grant me unwavering faith in you such that I am never afraid.

20

As soon as Jesus heard the word that was spoken, he saith...Be not afraid, only believe. (Mark 5:36)

Our Master lovingly asks us to have pure, childlike faith in him.

21

Now the God of hope fill you with all joy and peace in believing, that ye may abound in hope, through the power of the Holy Ghost. (Rom 15:13)

God, you take thousands of steps toward us when we begin on our first step of diligently seeking you.

22

...If ye have faith as a grain of mustard seed, ye shall say unto this mountain, Remove hence to yonder place; and it shall remove; and nothing shall be impossible unto you. (Matt 17:20)

Real faith in God Almighty, even a minute amount, removes obstacles because there is nothing impossible for him.

23

Let not your heart be troubled: ye believe in God, believe also in me....if I go and prepare a place for you, I will come again, and receive you unto myself;... (John 14:1, 3)

Our Redeemer asks us to believe firmly in his promises, even if it seems that much time lapses until they transpire.

24

Fight the good fight of faith, lay hold on eternal life, whereunto thou art also called.... (1 Tim 6:12)

To renounce God is spiritual death, but being steadfast in him leads to eternal life.

25

...Go thy way; and as thou hast believed, so be it done unto thee.... (Matt 8:13)

The Lord commends zealous faith and blesses us with his gift of peace.

26

Without faith it is impossible to please him: for he that cometh to God must believe that he is, and that he is a rewarder of them that diligently seek him. (Heb 11:6)

We can never benefit from an intimate relationship with God if we don't express or live our faith in him!

27

Let us draw near with a true heart in full assurance of faith, having our hearts sprinkled from an evil conscience.... (Heb 10:22)

Faith is meaningless if we don't forsake evil. Help our faith be meaningful.

28

...resist stedfast in the faith, knowing that the same afflictions are accomplished in your brethren that are in the world. (1 Pet 5:9)

Lord, only with you can we effectively resist the temptations of evil and destruction.

29

Continue in the faith grounded and settled, and be not moved away from the hope of the gospel.... (Col 1:23)

Perseverance in faith is essential if we want to be counted among the ever-living saints.

30

Remembering without ceasing your work of faith, and labour of love, and patience of hope.... (1 Thess 1:3)

Let our sincerity of faith lead to good deeds and life with a newness of spirit.

31

Here is the patience of the saints:...they that keep the commandments of God, and the faith of Jesus....Blessed are the dead which die in the Lord from henceforth: Yea, saith the Spirit, that they may rest.... (Rev 14:12, 13)

God, grant eternal rest to those who believe in judgment and live by your holy laws.

February

Trust and Hope

1

Blessed is the man that trusteth in the Lord, *and whose hope the* Lord *is. (Jer 17:7)*

One who trusts and hopes in God for everything correctly understands that the fountain of all goodness is the Lord.

2

For whatsoever things were written aforetime were written for our learning, that we through patience and comfort of the scriptures might have hope. (Rom 15:4)

God's living words impart the hope we need to strengthen our spiritual life.

3

Trust in the LORD, and do good; so shalt thou dwell in the land, and verily thou shalt be fed. (Ps 37:3)

Trust that God will bless us with his goodness and mercy.

4

Trust in the LORD with all thine heart; and lean not unto thine own understanding. In all thy ways acknowledge him, and he shall direct thy paths. (Prov 3:5, 6)

Foolish and self-robbed is he who seeks not God's guidance but relies solely on his wit and experience.

5

But I would not have you to be ignorant, brethren, concerning them which are asleep, that ye sorrow not, even as others which have no hope. For if we believe that Jesus died and rose again, even so them also which sleep in Jesus will God bring with him. (1 Thess 4:13, 14)

Sorrow for our dear departed ones may be for temporary separation, not the complete end of life, for there is the hope of resurrection and reunion.

6

Thus saith the Lord; *Cursed be the man that trusteth in man, and maketh flesh his arm, and whose heart departeth from the* Lord. *(Jer 17:5)*

Condemned to failure is the one who forsakes divine providence, but blessed is the individual who trusts in God.

7

Happy is he that hath the God of Jacob for his help, whose hope is in the Lord *his God. (Ps 146:5)*

Fully trusting in God's work for us behind the scenes gives us contentment about the present and future.

8

God is my salvation; I will trust, and not be afraid: for the Lord *JEHOVAH is my strength and my song; he also is become my salvation. (Isa 12:2)*

Wondrous is God in his deliverance of them who patiently trust him.

9

Behold, the eye of the Lord *is upon them that fear him, upon them that hope in his mercy. (Ps 33:18)*

With compassion, the Lord doesn't turn anyone away when he or she comes to him in prayer.

10

In God I will praise his word, in God I have put my trust; I will not fear what flesh can do unto me. (Ps 56:4)

We must trust in God's help, leaving all matters in his reliable hands.

11

Why art thou cast down, O my soul? and why art thou disquieted in me? hope thou in God: for I shall yet praise him for the help of his countenance. (Ps 42:5)

Allow the Lord's light to consume the darkness of despair; only then will you chant his praise.

12

He shall cover thee with his feathers, and under his wings shalt thou trust: his truth shall be thy shield and buckler. (Ps 91:4)

Where else could we go when life's circumstances seem frightening but the gentle arms of our heavenly Father!

13

Blessed be the God and Father of our Lord Jesus Christ, which according to his abundant mercy hath begotten us again unto a lively hope by the resurrection of Jesus Christ from the dead. (1 Pet 1:3)

Truly blessed is he who established our salvation, ever granting us hope of good things to come.

14

O taste and see that the LORD is good: blessed is the man that trusteth in him. (Ps 34:8)

Meditate on the Lord's goodness every day and the good things he brings into your life.

15

...hope in the LORD: *for with the* LORD *there is mercy, and with him is plenteous redemption. (Ps 130:7)*

Trust in the Lamb of God, who takes away the sins of the world and brings us spiritual freedom.

16

But let all those that put their trust in thee rejoice: let them ever shout for joy, because thou defendest them: let them also that love thy name be joyful in thee. (Ps 5:11)

From the beginning of the world, there has been no other God who acts mightily for the one who trusts him and does righteousness.

17

...but we know that, when he shall appear, we shall be like him;...And every man that hath this hope in him purifieth himself, even as he is pure. (1 John 3:2, 3)

Prepare yourself each day for the coming of the Lord through your words and deeds.

18

For thou art my hope, O Lord GOD: *thou art my trust from my youth. (Ps 71:5)*

Help us remember the hope and blessing you have given us throughout our life.

19

It is good that a man should both hope and quietly wait for the salvation of the LORD. *(Lam 3:26)*

True blessings come when we are patient and hopeful through times of trouble.

20

Offer the sacrifices of righteousness, and put your trust in the LORD. *(Ps 4:5)*

Help us fulfill our obligations, and surrender our trust to your will and plan for us.

21

And have hope toward God...that there shall be a resurrection of the dead,... (Acts 24:15)

Help us through this earthly existence to know the closeness of you, our Savior.

22

Commit thy way unto the LORD; *trust also in him; and he shall bring it to pass. (Ps 37:5)*

May we never doubt your wisdom, love, or ways because while you close some doors of opportunities, you always open better ones.

23

If in this life only we have hope in Christ, we are of all men most miserable. (1 Cor 15:19)

Our love for Christ gives our life meaning and purpose beyond this earthly existence.

24

Trust in him at all times; ye people, pour out your heart before him: God is a refuge for us. (Ps 62:8)

Turn to God in times of need and trust in his limitless love.

25

The LORD *taketh pleasure in them that fear him, in those that hope in his mercy. (Ps 147:11)*

The infinite mercy of the Lord is impossible to fathom and our response is one of awe!

26

Charge them that are rich in this world, that they be not high-minded, nor trust in uncertain riches, but in the living God, who giveth us richly all things to enjoy. (1 Tim 6:17)

Trust in God whose riches are spiritually eternal.

27

We had the sentence of death in ourselves, that we should not trust in ourselves, but in God which raiseth the dead. (2 Cor 1:9)

The Lord overcame sin by his death and granted us spiritual life through his resurrection.

28

Be of good courage, and he shall strengthen your heart, all ye that hope in the LORD. (Ps 31:24)

May God, the hope of all the earth, be our protector, safe haven, close companion, and guide.

29

And there is hope in thine end, saith the LORD.... (Jer 31:17)

Our hope comes from the Lord, who holds all things in the palms of his hands.

March

Forgiveness

1

Repent therefore of this thy wickedness, and pray God, if perhaps the thought of thine heart may be forgiven thee. (Acts 8:22)

Lead a life of continual repentance worthy of God's forgiveness.

2

For thou, Lord, art good, and ready to forgive; and plenteous in mercy unto all them that call upon thee. (Ps 86:5)

God extends his promise of forgiveness as encouragement for our repentance.

3

Look upon mine affliction and my pain; and forgive all my sins. (Ps 25:18)

The righteous may repeatedly fall in sin but quickly arise every time. Lord, with your grace, I will overcome sin.

4

If we confess our sins, he is faithful and just to forgive us our sins, and to cleanse us from all unrighteousness. (1 John 1:9)

God's forgiveness and mercy wash us clean of our sins.

5

Hearken therefore unto the supplications of thy servant...and when thou hearest, forgive. (2 Chr 6:21)

Ask God's forgiveness as the first of all your requests.

6

Blessed is he whose transgression is forgiven, whose sin is covered. (Ps 32:1)

God, help us to recognize our sins and not repeat them.

7

If thou, LORD, shouldest mark iniquities, O LORD, who shall stand? But there is forgiveness with thee, that thou mayest be feared. (Ps 130:3, 4)

God will not turn us away when we sincerely seek his forgiveness, no matter the magnitude of our sins.

8

It may be that the house of Judah will hear all the evil which I purpose to do unto them; that they may return every man from his evil way; that I may forgive their iniquity and their sin. (Jer 36:3)

The Lord intends not to destroy, but to return the lost to his bosom.

9

Then said Jesus, Father, forgive them; for they know not what they do.... (Luke 23:34)

May this be our prayer in all our relationships.

10

...be of good cheer; thy sins be forgiven thee.
(Matt 9:2)

It is a contrite heart that allows the Lord's forgiveness to enter.

11

Wherefore I say unto you, All manner of sin
and blasphemy shall be forgiven unto men: but
the blasphemy against the Holy Ghost shall not
be forgiven unto men. (Matt 12:31)

The Holy Spirit works in us to help us realize
our sins. Always be open to the work of the
Holy Spirit in your life.

12

To the Lord our God belong mercies and for-
givenesses, though we have rebelled against
him. (Dan 9:9)

The Lord is always forgiving and rich in mercy;
make me aware of my faults.

13

Bless the LORD, *O my soul, and forget not all his benefits: Who forgiveth all thine iniquities; who healeth all thy diseases. (Ps 103:2, 3)*

Focus not on any weakness or sin, but glorify God who crowns you every day with his loving kindness and tender mercies.

14

But that ye may know that the Son of man hath power on earth to forgive sins…. (Mark 2:10)

Christ our God is the forgiver, then, now, and forever as his Holy Spirit works through us to loosen every bond of sin.

15

Him hath God exalted with his right hand to be a Prince and a Saviour, for to give repentance…and forgiveness of sins. (Acts 5:31)

Oh Lord, help us to offer acceptable fruits of repentance unto everlasting life!

16

...to turn them from darkness to light, and from the power of Satan unto God, that they may receive forgiveness of sins, and inheritance among them which are sanctified by faith that is in me. (Acts 26:18)

The Lord does not desire the death of a sinner, but rather invites us to live in holiness.

17

...thou hast in love to my soul delivered it from the pit of corruption: for thou hast cast all my sins behind thy back. (Isa 38:17)

God gladly forgets my sin and draws me to a deeper love through repentance.

18

Thou hast forgiven the iniquity of thy people, thou hast covered all their sin. (Ps 85:2)

The Lord clothed us with his robe of righteousness through his bareness on the cross.

19

...They that are whole have no need of the physician, but they that are sick: I came not to call the righteous, but sinners to repentance. (Mark 2:17)

The Lord came to make the weak strong.

20

...we have redemption through his blood, the forgiveness of sins, according to the riches of his grace. (Eph 1:7)

The grandeur of God's grace is remarkable, like the forgiveness granted to the prodigal son.

21

I have blotted out, as a thick cloud, thy transgressions, and, as a cloud, thy sins: return unto me; for I have redeemed thee. (Isa 44:22)

In the great mercy of our Savior, the Sun of Righteousness, he wipes away the gloominess of all sin, to establish forgiveness, redemption, and hope for mankind.

22

And when ye stand praying, forgive, if ye have ought against any: that your Father also which is in heaven may forgive you your trespasses. (Mark 11:25)

I cannot approach God with any request, especially for his pity, if I myself do not pardon others.

23

And his lord was wroth, and delivered him to the tormentors....So likewise shall my heavenly Father do also unto you, if ye from your hearts forgive not every one his brother their trespasses. (Matt 18:34, 35)

Forgiving from the heart means completely forgetting the past and not holding a grudge, even if new offenses arise.

24

And forgive us our debts, as we forgive our debtors. (Matt 6:12)

Boldly seek God's mercy only after fulfilling the commandment of forgiving others.

25

Forbearing one another, and forgiving one another, if any man have a quarrel against any: even as Christ forgave you, so also do ye. (Col 3:13)

Since God forgives my many sins every day, shouldn't it be easy to forgive my fellow human beset by weakness as myself?

26

Then came Peter to him, and said, "Lord, how oft shall my brother sin against me, and I forgive him? till seven times?" Jesus saith unto him, "I say not unto thee, 'Until seven times': but, 'Until seventy times seven.'" (Matt 18:21, 22)

Forgive anyone who fails to do good or is truly sorry for committing evil, even if you know that there will be a reoccurrence.

27

Judge not, and ye shall not be judged: condemn not, and ye shall not be condemned: forgive, and ye shall be forgiven. (Luke 6:37)

Never forget that you are held accountable before the heavenly Judge for everything regarding yourself, including interaction with others.

28

Take heed to yourselves: If thy brother trespass against thee, rebuke him; and if he repent, forgive him. (Luke 17:3)

Always forgive and give others the chance to change.

29

And be ye kind one to another, tenderhearted, forgiving one another, even as God for Christ's sake hath forgiven you. (Eph 4:32)

What value is there in contemplating the Lord's sacrifice for our forgiveness if we don't practice his example of forgiving?

30

...Know therefore that God exacts from you less than your iniquity deserves. (Job 11:6)

God merely seeks our repentance as the basis for obtaining forgiveness.

31

For if ye forgive men their trespasses, your heavenly Father will also forgive you. But if ye forgive not men their trespasses, neither will your Father forgive your trespasses. (Matt 6:14, 15)

Tears of remorse for our own sins will achieve nothing if we don't forgive others.

April

Strength and Courage

1

...be strong in the Lord, and in the power of his might. Put on the whole armour of God, that ye may be able to stand against the wiles of the devil. (Eph 6:10, 11)

The spiritual strength that God gives is through knowing his truth, having faith, working for salvation, carrying the cross, and living the scriptures.

2

...be strong...be strong,...and be strong, all ye people of the land, saith the LORD, and work: for I am with you.... (Hagg 2:4)

Our strength comes from knowing that he is with us.

3

Say to them that are of a fearful heart, Be strong, fear not: behold, your God will come with...a recompense; he will come and save you. (Isa 35:4)

Directly to our hearts, God pledges his help though he may purposely linger to strengthen us through ardent prayer. Stay strong and fear not, for the Lord is near at hand.

4

I can do all things through Christ which strengtheneth me. (Phil 4:13)

By him I will perform what's impossible for me and succeed.

5

They that wait upon the LORD shall renew their strength; they shall mount up with wings as eagles.... (Isa 40:31)

God's people rise high as eagles above problems.

6

...My grace is sufficient for thee: for my strength is made perfect in weakness. Most gladly therefore will I rather glory in my infirmities, that the power of Christ may rest upon me. (2 Cor 12:9)

For the humble person, the moment of most weakness is also the moment of most divine support.

7

Fear thou not; for I am with thee: be not dismayed; for I am thy God: I will strengthen thee; yea, I will help thee; yea, I will uphold thee with the right hand of my righteousness. (Isa 41:10)

Whenever we feel helpless and hopeless, remember God's supporting words because he extends his right arm of power to prevent our fall.

8

Be strong and of a good courage, fear not, nor be afraid of them: for the LORD thy God, he it is that doth go with thee; he will not fail thee, nor forsake thee. (Deut 31:6)

A true Christian relies solely on God's help, not human might or intelligence.

9

...O man greatly beloved, fear not: peace be unto thee, be strong, yea, be strong. And when he had spoken unto me, I was strengthened.... (Dan 10:19)

God's word gives us strength, takes away our fear, and brings us peace.

10

Therefore shall ye keep all the commandments which I command you this day, that ye may be strong.... (Deut 11:8)

I cannot expect to gain God's strength if I don't fulfill what he asks of me.

11

Wait on the LORD: be of good courage, and he shall strengthen thine heart: wait, I say, on the LORD. (Ps 27:14)

It is through patience that we will find strength.

12

Be ye therefore very courageous to keep and to do all that is written in the book of the law of Moses, that ye turn not aside therefrom to the right hand or to the left. (Josh 23:6)

The path of God requires courage and perseverance.

13

The righteous also shall hold on his way, and he that hath clean hands shall be stronger and stronger. (Job 17:9)

Divine assistance is obtainable by no other means except by keeping oneself far from wickedness.

14

My flesh and my heart faileth: but God is the strength of my heart, and my portion for ever. (Ps 73:26)

Focusing on a problem's magnitude causes depression, but the Lord's strong arm always pulls us upward.

15

For when we were yet without strength, in due time Christ died for the ungodly. (Rom 5:6)

The Savior strengthened us to rise from our fall.

16

In the day when I cried thou answeredst me, and strengthenedst me with strength in my soul. (Ps 138:3)

Be grateful for the miraculous strength God provided us to handle arduous problems.

17

He giveth power to the faint; and to them that have no might he increaseth strength. (Isa 40:29)

The feeble are strengthened and the endangered are protected by the Lord of heaven and earth.

18

The LORD is my strength and my shield; my heart trusted in him, and I am helped: therefore my heart greatly rejoiceth; and with my song will I praise him. (Ps 28:7)

With confidence, we live and give praise to the Almighty.

19

...there be more with us than with him: With him is an arm of flesh; but with us is the LORD our God to help us, and to fight our battles.... (2 Chr 32:7, 8)

Invisible to us, God strengthens us with countless angelic warriors against the enemies seeking to devour us.

20

But be not thou far from me, O LORD: O my strength, haste thee to help me. (Ps 22:19)

What a wonderful, humble prayer that swiftly beckons the merciful Savior for our intervention!

21

The LORD *is my light and my salvation; whom shall I fear? the* LORD *is the strength of my life; of whom shall I be afraid? (Ps 27:1)*

Who can stand against us if God is on our side?

22

Unto thee, O my strength, will I sing: for God is my defence, and the God of my mercy. (Ps 59:17)

Mercifully, the heavenly Father defends us from those things that seek to destroy us.

23

God is my strength and power: and he maketh my way perfect. (2 Sam 22:33)

With God, I have all that I need.

24

In God is my salvation and my glory: the rock of my strength, and my refuge, is in God. (Ps 62:7)

It is in God that we find our strength and purpose—not in what we do or how much we own.

25

...in thine hand it is to make great, and to give strength unto all. (1 Chr 29:12)

All blessings, spiritual and materialistic, are from God. All other sources are finite if not even fake.

26

Be ye strong therefore, and let not your hands be weak: for your work shall be rewarded. (2 Chr 15:7)

If God is promising rewards and providing the strength to work, will there be any excuse for laziness?

27

Be of good courage, and let us behave ourselves valiantly for our people, and for the cities of our God: and let the LORD *do that which is good in his sight. (1 Chr 19:13)*

The Lord bestows his grace if we bravely set a good example in society and stand for what is right and just.

28

*For thou hast girded me with strength to battle:
them that rose up against me hast thou subdued
under me. (2 Sam 22:40)*

God is my strength in all the battles that life
presents.

29

*The LORD is their strength, and he is the saving
strength of his anointed. (Ps 28:8)*

It is in knowing the Lord that we are made
strong and find our shelter.

30

*But the God of all grace, who hath called us
unto his eternal glory by Christ Jesus, after that
ye have suffered a while, make you perfect, stablish, strengthen, settle you. (1 Pet 5:10)*

Honor and glory undeniably come after steady
spiritual dedication throughout life.

May

Fear Not

1

Thou drewest near in the day that I called upon thee: Thou saidst, Fear not. (Lam 3:57)

More than 365 times throughout the Bible, God asks us not to fear, be afraid, or be frightened because he protects us every day.

2

...Fear thou not...Let not thine hands be slack. The LORD thy God in the midst of thee is mighty; he will save, he will rejoice over thee with joy; he will rest in his love, he will joy over thee with singing. (Zeph 3:16, 17)

The Lord dwells in our hearts vanquishing fear. He rejoices over us as a father loves to see his children near him.

3

The LORD appeared unto him the same night, and said, I am the God of Abraham thy father: fear not, for I am with thee, and will bless thee.... (Gen 26:24)

If my Lord is the God of everything and all before me, I should fear nothing and no one!

4

That he would grant unto us, that we being delivered out of the hand of our enemies might serve him without fear, in holiness and righteousness before him, all the days of our life. (Luke 1:74, 75)

Wonderfully, the Lord paves the path for worshiping him throughout life, at which end we shouldn't fear death because it brings us closer to him who died for us.

5

...Fear not: for they that be with us are more than they that be with them...and, behold, the mountain was full of horses and chariots of fire round about Elisha. (2 Kgs 6:16, 17)

God quiets every fear that we encounter.

6

Fear not, little flock; for it is your Father's good pleasure to give you the kingdom. (Luke 12:32)

The Shepherd comes to comfort, not rebuke. What's better, to be on his shoulders or remain in thorns?

7

Then shalt thou prosper, if thou takest heed to fulfill the statutes...dread not, nor be dismayed. (1 Chr 22:13)

We become stronger and need not fear our enemies when we enter the relationship God wants with us.

8

Though I walk through the valley of the shadow of death, I will fear no evil: for thou art with me…. (Ps 23:4)

Even surrounded by threats, no danger can frighten me when I make the Lord my shelter.

9

Ye have not received the spirit of bondage again to fear; but ye have received the Spirit of adoption, whereby we cry, Abba, Father. (Rom 8:15)

We are children of the peace-giver and can call on the Father at all times.

10

…Fear not: for God is come to prove you, and that his fear may be before your faces, that ye sin not. (Exod 20:20)

Be not afraid of tribulations. Instead, seek God's help, forsake sin, and look to him who will lead you to life everlasting.

11

Thus saith the LORD *that created thee...that formed thee...Fear not: for I have redeemed thee, I have called thee by thy name; thou art mine. (Isa 43:1)*

The Shepherd knows us individually because each of us is precious in his eyes.

12

But and if ye suffer for righteousness' sake, happy are ye: and be not afraid...be ready always to give an answer to every man that asketh you a reason of the hope that is in you.... (1 Pet 3:14, 15)

Without complaining about any sufferings, stand unafraid to declare your faith in him.

13

...ye approach this day unto battle against your enemies: let not your hearts faint, fear not, and do not tremble, neither be ye terrified.... (Deut 20:3)

If you are close to God, then you should fear nothing!

14

Fear ye not therefore, ye are of more value than many sparrows. (Matt 10:31)

Fear not being forgotten; God holds you very dear.

15

The LORD, he it is that doth go before thee; he will be with thee, he will not fail thee, neither forsake thee: fear not, neither be dismayed. (Deut 31:8)

Let these words resonate when you think life is becoming full of fear—someone intends to harm you or a small issue grows into a major problem.

16

...there shall no evil touch thee...neither shalt thou be afraid of destruction when it cometh. (Job 5:19, 21)

Upon encountering distress, I must not fear but surrender all to God's complete control.

17

...Be not afraid nor dismayed by reason of this great multitude; for the battle is not yours, but God's. (2 Chr 20:15)

If we are true to God, he will protect us from those who attack us.

18

...ye that know righteousness, the people in whose heart is my law; fear ye not the reproach of men, neither be ye afraid of their revilings. (Isa 51:7)

God is fearful to his enemies, but to his children he takes away fear and comforts them in times of need.

19

...Fear not...for from the first day that thou didst set thine heart to understand, and to chasten thyself before thy God, thy words were heard, and I am come for thy words. (Dan 10:12)

Caringly, God calms our fears, even through others, to help us persevere in our spiritual fervor toward heaven.

20

For I the LORD *thy God will hold thy right hand, saying unto thee, Fear not; I will help thee. (Isa 41:13)*

Believe that the Mighty Lord is actively resolving your problems and will give you timely success.

21

Ye shall not respect persons in judgment...ye shall not be afraid of the face of man; for the judgment is God's. (Deut 1:17)

In judging between right and wrong, fear not truth and justice regardless of who the wrongdoer might be.

22

Since thou wast precious in my sight, thou hast been honourable, and I have loved thee....Fear not: for I am with thee.... (Isa 43:4, 5)

He is with us, Emmanuel, and we need not fear any trial or doubt this.

23

And Jesus came and touched them, and said, Arise, and be not afraid. (Matt 17:7)

Gently, Lord, touch our hearts, especially when we realize our weaknesses.

24

...son of man, be not afraid of them, neither be afraid...be not afraid of their words, nor be dismayed at their looks.... (Ezek 2:6)

Be our strength and guide in all that we say and do.

25

Be not afraid of sudden fear, neither of the desolation of the wicked, when it cometh. For the LORD shall be thy confidence.... (Prov 3:25, 26)

Raise our spirits, Lord, in the midst of grief and worldly problems.

26

And fear not them which kill the body, but are not able to kill the soul: but rather fear him which is able to destroy both soul and body in hell. (Matt 10:28)

Strengthen and protect our soul, Lord, even though our flesh may be weak and perishing.

27

When a prophet speaketh in the name of the LORD, *if the thing follow not...the prophet hath spoken it presumptuously: thou shalt not be afraid of him. (Deut 18:22)*

Make us aware of your truth, Oh God, and not fall victim to false messages and prophets who will lead us astray.

28

Fear thou not...neither be dismayed...I will save thee...Jacob shall return, and shall be in rest, and be quiet, and none shall make him afraid. (Jer 30:10)

Cast out all fear, Oh Lord, and replace it with protection, well-being, and love.

29

...Fear not: ye have done all this wickedness: yet turn not aside from following the LORD, *but serve the* LORD *with all your heart. (1 Sam 12:20)*

Encourage us, Lord, to rely entirely on your word and guidance.

30

For God hath not given us the spirit of fear; but of power, and of love, and of a sound mind. (2 Tim 1:7)

God, you overcame sin and death so that we might be free and no longer live in fear.

31

Fear none of those things which thou shalt suf-fer...be thou faithful unto death, and I will give thee a crown of life. (Rev 2:10)

Lord, do not abandon your servant in crisis, but give hope and patience to endure what lies ahead.

June

Prayer

1

If my people, which are called by my name, shall humble themselves, and pray, and seek my face, and turn from their wicked ways; then will I hear from heaven, and will forgive their sin, and will heal their land. (2 Chr 7:14)

Oh merciful Lord, grant us a contrite heart.

2

In my distress I called upon the LORD, and cried to my God: and he did hear my voice out of his temple, and my cry did enter into his ears. (2 Sam 22:7)

Lord, help us to turn every problem, frustration, worry, shortcoming, and desire into heartfelt prayer.

3

And it came to pass, when I heard these words, that I sat down and wept, and mourned certain days, and fasted, and prayed before the God of heaven. (Neh 1:4)

Loving God, help me to see you as the one who sustains and nourishes me.

4

As for me, I will call upon God; and the LORD shall save me. Evening, and morning, and at noon, will I pray, and cry aloud: and he shall hear my voice. (Ps 55:16, 17)

Make time out of your busy schedule to establish a deep relationship with God.

5

Blessed be God, which hath not turned away my prayer, nor his mercy from me. (Ps 66:20)

God is never too busy to hear you. You just need to set the time, place, and duration.

6

...but I give myself unto prayer. (Ps 109:4)

Lord, help me to lean on you instead of facing enemies, difficulties, and temptations all alone.

7

I love the LORD, because he hath heard my voice and my supplications. (Ps 116:1)

As a compassionate Father, the Lord welcomes his children into his arms to voice anything with him.

8

Then shall ye call upon me, and ye shall go and pray unto me, and I will hearken unto you. (Jer 29:12)

Prayer is connection with God; the more time we stay with him, the more we become like him and want to be with him.

9

And I set my face unto the Lord God, to seek by prayer and supplications, with fasting, and sackcloth, and ashes. (Dan 9:3)

Lord God, help me to amend my ways and turn to you through prayer and fasting.

10

But thou, when thou prayest, enter into thy closet, and when thou hast shut thy door, pray to thy Father which is in secret; and thy Father which seeth in secret shall reward thee openly. (Matt 6:6)

May every room be sanctified by the very presence of God when we speak privately with him, such that our dwellings become houses of prayer, purity, and blessings.

11

Howbeit this kind [of demon] goeth not out but by prayer and fasting. (Matt 17:21)

The Lord himself taught us to fight devils by beckoning God's help through pure prayer and fasting.

12

Watch and pray, that ye enter not into temptation: the spirit indeed is willing, but the flesh is weak. (Matt 26:41)

Lord, guide me in the way of prayer to that I will grow strong in your love.

13

Jesus answering saith unto them, Have faith in God....Therefore I say unto you, What things soever ye desire, when ye pray, believe that ye receive them, and ye shall have them. (Mark 11:22, 24)

May I come to know you more intimately and gain a clean heart through prayer.

14

And it came to pass, that, as he was praying in a certain place, when he ceased, one of his disciples said unto him, Lord, teach us to pray.... (Luke 11:1)

Lord, teach me the language of prayer so that I may abide in you.

15

And he said unto them, When ye pray, say, Our Father which art in heaven, Hallowed be thy name. Thy kingdom come. Thy will be done, as in heaven, so in earth. (Luke 11:2)

Lord God, help me to accept your holy will as one who works nothing but the best for me.

16

And he spake a parable unto them to this end, that men ought always to pray, and not to faint. (Luke 18:1)

How natural it is to despair when things don't go your way, but against all pessimism persist in your prayers, even for expressing your frustrations with God's plans.

17

And shall not God avenge his own elect, which cry day and night unto him, though he bear long with them? I tell you that he will avenge them speedily. Nevertheless when the Son of man cometh, shall he find faith on the earth? (Luke 18:7, 8)

God always hears your prayers and rescues his faithful.

18

Watch ye therefore, and pray always, that ye may be accounted worthy to escape all these things that shall come to pass, and to stand before the Son of man. (Luke 21:36)

Come to my aid, Oh God, and help me recognize your presence in my life.

19

I pray not that thou shouldest take them out of the world, but that thou shouldest keep them from the evil. (John 17:15)

Deliver us, Lord, from all evils.

20

And when they had prayed, the place was shaken where they were assembled together; and they were all filled with the Holy Ghost, and they spake the word of God with boldness. (Acts 4:31)

Send us your Spirit, Oh Lord, and renew the face of the earth.

21

Likewise the Spirit also helpeth our infirmities: for we know not what we should pray for as we ought: but the Spirit itself maketh intercession for us with groanings which cannot be uttered. (Rom 8:26)

When words cannot express grief or joy, God's Holy Spirit unites with us to connect with him who shares our sorrows and celebrations.

22

Praying always with all prayer and supplication in the Spirit, and watching thereunto with all perseverance and supplication.... (Eph 6:18)

Bless us, Lord, that we may experience your presence.

23

When my soul fainted within me I remembered the LORD: and my prayer came in unto thee, into thine holy temple. (Jonah 2:7)

My Lord Jesus Christ, have mercy on me, a sinner.

24

Rejoice in the LORD always. Again I will say rejoice. Be anxious for nothing but in every thing by prayer and supplication with thanksgiving let your requests be made known unto God. (Phil 4:4, 6)

Knock and the door will always be opened.

25

Is any among you afflicted? let him pray. Is any merry? let him sing psalms. (Jas 5:13)

If you are in anguish, pray more earnestly; if you are joyful, praise God with chants of veneration.

26

Confess your faults one to another, and pray one for another, that ye may be healed. The effectual fervent prayer of a righteous man availeth much. (Jas 5:16)

Help us, Lord, to love and pray for one another.

27

I exhort therefore, that, first of all, supplications, prayers, intercessions, and giving of thanks, be made for all men. (1 Tim 2:1)

Help us, Lord, to be instruments of your love and mercy.

28

For the eyes of the Lord are over the righteous, and his ears are open unto their prayers: but the face of the Lord is against them that do evil. (1 Pet 3:12)

Hear our prayers, Oh God, and grant us our deepest desires.

29

And the smoke of the incense, which came with the prayers of the saints, ascended up before God out of the angel's hand. (Rev 8:4)

Like incense rising, may our prayers rise to the throne of the ever-loving God.

30

Yet the Lord *will command his lovingkindness in the day time, and in the night his song shall be with me, and my prayer unto the God of my life. (Ps 42:8)*

Lord, look with favor on us all each moment of the day.

July

Comfort and Reassurance

1

And call upon me in the day of trouble: I will deliver thee, and thou shalt glorify me. (Ps 50:15)

Lord, comfort us with the promise of certain rescue.

2

Wherefore comfort yourselves together, and edify one another, even as also ye do. (1 Thess 5:11)

Lord, your words comfort me in my weakness.

3

Let, I pray thee, thy merciful kindness be for my comfort, according to thy word unto thy servant. (Ps 119:76)

Merciful Lord, my heart is reassured by your words and promises.

4

Therefore take no thought, saying, What shall we eat? or, What shall we drink? or, Wherewithal shall we be clothed?...for your heavenly Father knoweth that ye have need of all these things. (Matt 6:31, 32)

Our reliance is on a tender Lord who takes care of all our physical and spiritual needs before we ask about them.

5

Say ye to the righteous, that it shall be well with him: for they shall eat the fruit of their doings. (Isa 3:10)

The Lord assures us that the righteous will ultimately prevail.

6

...lo, I am with you always, even unto the end of the world. Amen. (Matt 28:20)

With full assurance that he ever dwells in our hearts, amid us, and around us, he is truly Emmanuel.

7

And it shall come to pass, that before they call, I will answer; and while they are yet speaking, I will hear. (Isa 65:24)

God knows what we'll request because he knows us more than we know ourselves.

8

...upon this rock I will build my church; and the gates of hell shall not prevail against it. (Matt 16:18)

Lord, strengthen us with your power, and make us firm in our faith.

9

As one whom his mother comforteth, so will I comfort you; and ye shall be comforted.... (Isa 66:13)

Like a caring parent, God comforts his people throughout life's daily struggles.

10

Come unto me, all ye that labour and are heavy laden, and I will give you rest. Take my yoke upon you, and learn of me; for I am meek and lowly in heart: and ye shall find rest unto your souls. (Matt 11:28, 29)

Thank you, Lord, for comforting us and providing rest for our souls.

11

For since the beginning of the world men have not heard, nor perceived by the ear, neither hath the eye seen, O God, beside thee, what he hath prepared for him that waiteth for him. Thou meetest him that rejoiceth and worketh righteousness.... (Isa 64:4, 5)

There is no God other than our Lord, who has many wonderful surprises for his beloved children.

12

...With men it is impossible, but not with God: for with God all things are possible. (Mark 10:27)

Lord, with you I can overcome all problems that trouble me. Thank you.

13

Behold, I am the LORD, *the God of all flesh: is there any thing too hard for me? (Jer 32:27)*

Without you, Lord, even the simplest things are difficult; yet with you everything is possible.

14

He that overcometh, the same shall be clothed in white raiment; and I will not blot out his name out of the book of life, but I will confess his name before my Father, and before his angels. (Rev 3:5)

You are my Lord! In you I rest my soul.

15

And the LORD *said unto Satan, The* LORD *rebuke thee, O Satan; even the* LORD.... *(Zech 3:2)*

Help me, Lord, to turn to you, and protect me from all that is evil and destructive.

16

Being confident of this very thing, that he which hath begun a good work in you will perform it until the day of Jesus Christ. (Phil 1:6)

Strengthen my faith so that it may permeate all my actions.

17

Can a woman forget her sucking child, that she should not have compassion on the son of her womb? yea, they may forget, yet will I not forget thee. (Isa 49:15)

Lord, you never forget me. Help me to be always mindful of your presence in my life.

18

...I am the resurrection, and the life: he that believeth in me, though he were dead, yet shall he live. (John 11:25)

Our time will unquestionably come to leave the world, yet God's comfort for us and our beloved departed ones is the new life with Christ.

19

...The beloved of the LORD shall dwell in safety by him; and the LORD shall cover him all the day long, and he shall dwell between his shoulders. (Deut 33:12)

Never worry about anything, but rather boldly face all circumstances in life with the comfort of God's love.

20

...where sin abounded, grace did much more abound: That as sin hath reigned unto death, even so might grace reign through righteousness unto eternal life by Jesus Christ our Lord. (Rom 5:20, 21)

Though you may resist temptation but still fall, look to God's comforting grace, which shall grant you victory in due time.

21

I have set the LORD always before me: because he is at my right hand, I shall not be moved. Therefore my heart is glad, and my glory rejoiceth: my flesh also shall rest in hope. (Ps 16:8, 9)

May you, Oh Lord, always be my focus in all the challenges I face.

22

And we know that all things work together for good to them that love God, to them who are the called according to his purpose. (Rom 8:28)

Don't be glum or let despair seep in. Rather, be absolutely sure that God is planning the very best, and you will soon experience his miracles.

23

Thou, which hast shewed me great and sore troubles, shalt quicken me again, and shalt bring me up again from the depths of the earth. Thou shalt increase my greatness, and comfort me on every side. (Ps 71:20, 21)

Oh God, comfort me in my suffering, rejoice with me in my victories.

24

But as it is written, Eye hath not seen, nor ear heard, neither have entered into the heart of man, the things which God hath prepared for them that love him. (1 Cor 2:9)

Lord, help me to love you more dearly so that I can see and hear you more clearly.

25

Remember the word unto thy servant, upon which thou hast caused me to hope. This is my comfort in my affliction: for thy word hath quickened me. (Ps 119:49, 50)

Your comforting words bring consolation and settle our emotions.

26

Blessed be God, even the Father of our Lord Jesus Christ, the Father of mercies, and the God of all comfort; Who comforteth us in all our tribulation, that we may be able to comfort them which are in any trouble, by the comfort wherewith we ourselves are comforted of God. (2 Cor 1:3, 4)

Real and lasting comfort comes from the One who's able to pour it abundantly into our hearts.

27

I the LORD have called thee in righteousness, and will hold thine hand, and will keep thee.... (Isa 42:6)

Lord, guide me with your reassuring hand through every step of my life.

28

Now our Lord Jesus Christ himself, and God, even our Father, which hath loved us, and hath given us everlasting consolation and good hope through grace, Comfort your hearts, and stablish you in every good word and work. (2 Thess 2:16, 17)

God, console us in our steadfastness and encourage us along the path that leads to heaven.

29

And even to your old age I am he; and even to gray hairs will I carry you: I have made, and I will bear; even I will carry, and will deliver you. (Isa 46:4)

Rest assured in God's abilities, not your own, for he will carry you as his child even during your latter days.

30

...If God be for us, who can be against us? He that spared not his own Son, but delivered him up for us all, how shall he not with him also freely give us all things? (Rom 8:31, 32)

Lord, your gifts are immeasurable. How can I not respond with love?

31

And God shall wipe away all tears from their eyes; and there shall be no more death, neither sorrow, nor crying, neither shall there be any more pain: for the former things are passed away. (Rev 21:3, 4)

Compassionate God, you comfort us in times of death and sorrow; we rejoice in your love.

August

Peace

1

Peace I leave with you, My peace I give unto you: not as the world giveth, give I unto you. Let not your heart be troubled, neither let it be afraid. (John 14:27)

Oh King of Peace, grant us your unshaken, heavenly peace.

2

The peace of God, which passeth all understanding, shall keep your hearts and minds through Christ Jesus. (Phil 4:7)

God's peace keeps us from being overwhelmed by life's challenges.

3

He was wounded for our transgressions, he was bruised for our iniquities: the chastisement of our peace was upon him; and with his stripes we are healed. (Isa 53:5)

Through the passions of Christ we enjoy eternal peace.

4

Now the Lord of peace himself give you peace always by all means. The Lord be with you all. (2 Thess 3:16)

We need your presence and peace every moment, Lord.

5

I will give peace in the land, and ye shall lie down, and none shall make you afraid…. (Lev 26:6)

Settle our souls with your peace, Oh God, wherever we live.

6

The LORD will give strength unto his people; the LORD will bless his people with peace. (Ps 29:11)

Unite yourself with the Father of peace and enjoy his serenity and strength.

7

Glory to God in the highest, and on earth peace, good will toward men. (Luke 2:14)

We thank you Lord and humbly ask for your peace among us.

8

For I know the thoughts that I think toward you, saith the LORD, *thoughts of peace, and not of evil, to give you an expected end. (Jer 29:11)*

God's intentions are peaceful toward us, not for punishment.

9

...Jesus himself stood in the midst of them, and saith unto them, Peace be unto you. (Luke 24:36)

God, take charge of my life and put your peace in my heart.

10

...Peace, peace to him that is far off, and to him that is near, saith the LORD; *and I will heal him. (Isa 57: 19)*

Lord, bring me ever closer to you and to experience your unmatched peace.

11

These things I have spoken unto you, that in me ye might have peace. In the world ye shall have tribulation: but be of good cheer; I have overcome the world. (John 16:33)

Our Savior solves our problems so that we remain undisturbed in his peace.

12

...my kindness shall not depart from thee, neither shall the covenant of my peace be removed, saith the LORD that hath mercy on thee. (Isa 54:10)

I am grateful for your benevolence and tranquility, Oh my God.

13

Glory, honour, and peace, to every man that worketh good.... (Rom 2:10)

My Lord, you are the one who graciously helps and blesses me with all goodness.

14

The LORD lift up his countenance upon thee, and give thee peace. (Num 6:26)

Let us invite God's peace to calm our unstable and violent world.

15

I will both lay me down in peace, and sleep: for thou, LORD, only makest me dwell in safety. (Ps 4:8)

I will not worry, but leave all my problems in your good hands, Lord.

16

For unto us a child is born, unto us a son is given: and the government shall be upon his shoulder: and his name shall be called Wonderful, Counsellor, The mighty God, The everlasting Father, The Prince of Peace. (Isa 9:6)

My Lord, Jesus, I am forever grateful for your heavenly gift of peace.

17

The meek shalt inherit the earth; and shalt delight themselves in the abundance of peace. (Ps 37:11)

Make my heart serene and humble like yours, Lord.

18

*L*ORD, *thou wilt ordain peace for us: for thou also hast wrought all our works in us. (Isa 26:12)*

Seek God's help to accomplish your dreams and you will find his support.

19

The work of righteousness shall be peace; and the effect of righteousness quietness and assurance for ever. (Isa 32:17)

Lord, help me fulfill your commandments for my benefit.

20

My covenant [is] with him of life and peace.... (Mal 2:5)

With God's tranquillity and promises, we rejoice even amid challenges.

21

Through the tender mercy of our God;...to give light to them that sit in darkness and in the shadow of death, to guide our feet into the way of peace. (Luke 1:78, 79)

Good Savior, enlighten and keep me in your heavenly peace.

...Grace be unto you, and peace, from him which is, and which was, and which is to come; and from the seven Spirits which are before his throne. (Rev 1:4)

Oh heavenly king, grant me needed grace and peace.

Great peace have they which love thy law: and nothing shalt offend them. (Ps 119:165)

Living by God's commandments has its blessings and rewards.

My people shall dwell in a peaceable habitation, and in sure dwellings, and in quiet resting places. (Isa 32:18)

Lead me to inner calmness, Oh Shepherd, especially during my troubles.

I will hear what God the LORD will speak: for he will speak peace unto his people, and to his saints.... (Ps 85:8)

God's mercy and peace are confirmed mightily within us.

26

For ye shalt go out with joy, and be led forth with peace…. (Isa 55:12)

God, give me your peace while I'm away from home that I may return with all well-being.

27

Thou wilt keep him in perfect peace, whose mind is stayed on thee: because he trusteth in thee. (Isa 26:3)

Keep us in your faith, Oh Lord, and grant us your peace unto the end.

28

Grace and peace be multiplied unto you through the knowledge of God, and of Jesus our Lord. (2 Pet 1:2)

Living by the scriptures leads to peace with God and people.

29

…the battle bow shall be cut off: and he shall speak peace unto the nations…. (Zech 9:10)

Lord, let love, peace, and respect characterize all our relationships.

30

The LORD shall fight for you, and ye shall hold your peace. (Exod 14:14)

Preserve my patience and serenity while you handle all my problems, Lord.

31

Therefore being justified by faith, we have peace with God through our Lord Jesus Christ. (Rom 5:1)

Glory is to the Holy Trinity who established peace with mankind.

September

Wisdom

1

For the LORD *giveth wisdom: out of his mouth cometh knowledge and understanding. (Prov 2:6)*

Seek God's wisdom and guidance in the holy scriptures.

2

That the God of our Lord Jesus Christ, the Father of glory, may give unto you the spirit of wisdom and revelation in the knowledge of him. (Eph 1:17)

Lord, give me spiritual insight to realize your presence in my life.

3

The fear of the LORD *is the beginning of wisdom: a good understanding have all they that do his commandments: his praise endureth for ever. (Ps 111:10)*

Wisdom is attained by respecting God and obeying his laws.

4

See then that ye walk circumspectly, not as fools, but as wise,...Wherefore be ye not unwise, but understanding what the will of the Lord is. (Eph 5:15, 17)

God, I need your wisdom to know your will in all circumstances.

5

So teach us to number our days, that we may apply our hearts unto wisdom. (Ps 90:12)

Prudent is the individual who is ready for the eternal life.

6

If any of you lack wisdom, let him ask of God, that giveth to all men liberally, and upbraideth not; and it shall be given him. (Jas 1:5)

I humbly ask you, Lord, for the wisdom that leads to salvation.

7

He that getteth wisdom loveth his own soul: he that keepeth understanding shall find good. (Prov 19:8)

Seeking true wisdom is actually coming closer to our all-wise God.

8

Who is a wise man and endued with knowledge among you? let him shew out of a good conversation his works with meekness of wisdom. (Jas 3:13)

Sound wisdom is manifest in decent behavior and kind words.

9

For God giveth to a man that is good in his sight wisdom, and knowledge, and joy.... (Eccl 2:26)

Lord, graciously help us be your devout worshipers.

10

The wisdom that is from above is first pure, then peaceable, gentle, and easy to be intreated, full of mercy and good fruits, without partiality, and without hypocrisy. (Jas 3:17)

God produces spiritual fruits in our lives when we pursue godly wisdom.

11

Wisdom crieth without; she uttereth her voice in the streets....But whoso hearkeneth unto me shall dwell safely, and shall be quiet from fear of evil. (Prov 1:20, 33)

Reward us, God, for seeking spiritual prudence.

12

Therefore whosoever heareth these sayings of mine, and doeth them, I will liken him unto a wise man, which built his house upon a rock. (Matt 7:24)

The wise heed God's words and hence evade loss.

13

They that be wise shall shine as the brightness of the firmament; and they that turn many to righteousness as the stars for ever and ever. (Dan 12:3)

How great is the eternal honor of the wise, who lead others to God!

14

Behold, I send you forth as sheep in the midst of wolves: be ye therefore wise as serpents, and harmless as doves. (Matt 10:16)

With prudence and gentleness, we could bring others to the Lord.

15

God said to Solomon, Because...thou hast not asked riches...nor the life of thine enemies, neither...long life...wisdom and knowledge is granted unto thee. (2 Chr 1:11, 12)

Lord, help us focus on what's more important than any worldly possession.

16

For I will give you a mouth and wisdom, which all your adversaries shall not be able to gainsay nor resist. (Luke 21:15)

God speaks through us when we witness to his truth.

17

...I would have you wise unto that which is good, and simple concerning evil. And the God of peace shall bruise Satan under your feet shortly.... (Rom 16:19, 20)

God, give us purity to avoid sin and wisdom to acquire virtues.

18

...be filled with the knowledge of his will in all wisdom and spiritual understanding. (Col 1:9)

Search the scriptures to learn and practice God's wise words.

19

The mouth of the righteous speaketh wisdom, and his tongue talketh of judgment. (Ps 37:30)

Lord, guide our ways toward repentance and the everlasting life.

20

Woe unto them that are wise in their own eyes, and prudent in their own sight! (Isa 5:21)

Let us follow divine wisdom rather than limited human intellect.

21

...Blessed be the name of God for ever and ever: for wisdom and might are his:...he giveth wisdom unto the wise, and knowledge to them that know understanding. (Dan 2:20, 21)

Whoever uses wisdom for God's glorification and is grateful for this gift will be given more.

22

Through wisdom is a house builded; and by understanding it is established....A wise man is strong; yea, a man of knowledge increaseth strength. (Prov 24:3, 5)

God, give us the knowledge to come ever closer to you.

23

My son, let not them depart from thine eyes: keep sound wisdom and discretion....When thou liest down, thou shalt not be afraid: yea, thou shalt lie down, and thy sleep shall be sweet. (Prov 3:21, 24)

Lord, guide me to make wise decisions, so that there is no regret.

24

Happy is the man that findeth wisdom, and the man that getteth understanding....Her ways are ways of pleasantness, and all her paths are peace. (Prov 3:13, 17)

God's wisdom gives joy and purpose to our lives.

25

Wisdom is the principal thing; therefore get wisdom: and with all thy getting get understanding. (Prov 4:7)

Those who diligently seek wisdom will find it running to them.

26

A prudent man foreseeth the evil, and hideth himself.... (Prov 22:3)

Lord, give me the willpower to flee all unrighteousness.

27

The law of the LORD is perfect, converting the soul: the testimony of the LORD is sure, making wise the simple. (Ps 19:7)

Spiritual maturity comes by faithfully fulfilling God's holy commandments.

28

And unto man he said, Behold, the fear of the LORD, that is wisdom; and to depart from evil is understanding. (Job 28:28)

God commends the wise who flee temptation in fierce resistance.

29

When wisdom entereth into thine heart, and knowledge is pleasant unto thy soul; discretion shall preserve thee, understanding shall keep thee. (Prov 2:10, 11)

Lord, give me spiritual and secular wisdom to handle life's challenges.

30

Howbeit we speak wisdom among them that are perfect: yet not the wisdom of this world,...we speak the wisdom of God in a mystery, even the hidden wisdom, which God ordained before the world unto our glory. (1 Cor 2:6, 7)

Let us wisely exhibit honorable morals indicative of our noble religion.

October

Love and Charity

1

For God so loved the world, that he gave his only begotten Son, that whosoever believeth in him should not perish, but have everlasting life. (John 3:16)

Redemption is the expression of God's unquenchable love for humans.

2

A new commandment I give unto you, That ye love one another; as I have loved you, that ye also love one another. (John 13:34)

Unite us with you, Lord, and one another with the love you command.

3

But I say unto you, Love your enemies, bless them that curse you, do good to them that hate you, and pray for them which despitefully use you, and persecute you. (Matt 5:44)

God, give us a loving heart toward our fellow human.

4

...what doth the LORD thy God require of thee, but to fear the LORD thy God, to walk in all his ways, and to love him, and to serve the LORD thy God with all thy heart and with all thy soul. (Deut 10:12)

Godly fear means mindfulness to pursue God's ways out of deep love for him.

5

There is no fear in love; but perfect love casteth out fear: because fear hath torment. He that feareth is not made perfect in love. (1 John 4:18)

Love toward God surpasses the immature spiritual level of dreading him.

6

If a man say, I love God, and hateth his brother, he is a liar: for he that loveth not his brother whom he hath seen, how can he love God whom he hath not seen? (1 John 4:20)

Sincere love for others is manifestation of our love toward God.

7

…let us not love in word, neither in tongue; but in deed and in truth. (1 John 3:18)

Loving and helping others are cures for egocentricity with sure heavenly rewards.

8

Jesus answered and said unto him, "If a man love me, he will keep my words: and my Father will love him, and we will come unto him, and make our abode with him." (John 14:23)

Lord, make my heart obedient and sanctified as your resting place.

9

*For the Father himself loveth you, because ye
have loved me, and have believed that I came
out from God. (John 16:27)*

Accepting the Lord Jesus Christ as the Lamb of
God is appreciating the Father's love and invit-
ing the work of his Holy Spirit.

10

*But God commendeth his love toward us, in
that, while we were yet sinners, Christ died for
us. (Rom 5:8)*

My Lord, how great is your love, valuing my
salvation worth your precious blood!

11

*Who shall separate us from the love of Christ?
shall tribulation, or distress, or persecution, or
famine, or nakedness, or peril, or sword?...Nay,
in all these things we are more than conquerors
through him that loved us. (Rom 8:35, 37)*

Nothing and no one can match or remove
God's love, poured generously into our hearts.

12

I am crucified with Christ: nevertheless I live;
yet not I, but Christ liveth in me: and the life
which I now live in the flesh I live by the faith
of the Son of God, who loved me, and gave
himself for me. (Gal 2:20)

God, help me live in holiness in response to
your love.

13

And above all these things put on charity,
which is the bond of perfectness. And let the
peace of God rule in your hearts, to the which
also ye are called in one body…. (Col 3:14, 15)

Lord, facilitate the way for us to love and serve
others.

14

And above all things have fervent charity
among yourselves: for charity shall cover the
multitude of sins. (1 Pet 4:8)

We should love and forgive each other as God
does with us.

15

Seeing ye have purified your souls in obeying the truth through the Spirit unto unfeigned love of the brethren, see that ye love one another with a pure heart fervently. (1 Pet 1:22)

Help us spread your love to everyone, Lord.

16

He brought me to the banqueting house, and his banner over me was love. (Song 2:4)

The Lord invites us to enjoy his love and abide in him.

17

Flee also youthful lusts: but follow righteousness, faith, charity, peace, with them that call on the Lord out of a pure heart. (2 Tim 2:22)

God, make us devoted to you, and to shun evil.

18

Now abideth faith, hope, charity, these three; but the greatest of these is charity. (1 Cor 13:13)

Love is greatest because it characterizes our compassionate God.

Charity suffereth long, and is kind; charity envieth not; charity vaunteth not itself, is not puffed up,...beareth all things, believeth all things, hopeth all things, endureth all things. (1 Cor 13:4, 7)

May all our relationships be exemplified by such pure love.

20

And thou shalt love the Lord thy God with all thy heart, and with all thy soul, and with all thy mind, and with all thy strength: this is the first commandment. And the second is like, namely this, Thou shalt love thy neighbour as thyself. There is none other commandment greater than these. (Mark 12:30, 31)

Lord, bring us close to you and each other in true love.

21

Herein is love, not that we loved God, but that he loved us, and sent his Son to be the propitiation for our sins. (1 John 4:10)

Fill my heart with your divine love, God, and not worldly desires.

22

And we have known and believed the love that God hath to us. God is love; and he that dwelleth in love dwelleth in God, and God in him. (1 John 4:16)

I run toward your open arms, my Lord, where I find rest in your love.

23

Because he hath set his love upon me, therefore will I deliver him: I will set him on high, because he hath known my name. (Ps 91:14)

The Lord lovingly takes us under his wings of protection and nurture.

24

I am my beloved's, and my beloved is mine.... (Song 6:3)

Savior, I give you all my heart for my life is empty without your love.

25

Behold, what manner of love the Father hath bestowed upon us, that we should be called the sons of God.... (1 John 3:1)

Father, I find myself embraced in your arms when I contemplate your benevolence.

26

But ye, beloved, building up yourselves on your most holy faith, praying in the Holy Ghost, keep yourselves in the love of God, looking for the mercy of our Lord Jesus Christ unto eternal life. (Jude 1:20, 21)

No harmful passion can overtake us if we keep ourselves in God's love.

27

Behold, I will make them of the synagogue of Satan,...to come and worship before thy feet, and to know that I have loved thee. (Rev 3:9)

Lord, it is your love, not my goodness, which raises me above enemies.

28

As many as I love, I rebuke and chasten: be zealous therefore, and repent. (Rev 3:19)

As a parent who corrects children out of love, so does the Lord desire our sanctification through continual repentance.

29

Jesus Christ, the faithful witness, the firstborn from the dead...who loved us and washed us from our sins in his own blood.... (Rev 1:5)

Lord, mercifully wash me clean from all my sins.

30

The LORD hath appeared of old unto me, saying, "Yea, I have loved thee with an everlasting love: therefore with lovingkindness have I drawn thee." (Jer 31:3)

Let us always enjoy God's unceasing love and be ever attached to him.

31

He that loveth father or mother more than me is not worthy of me: and he that loveth son or daughter more than me is not worthy of me. (Matt 10:37)

Lord, let no relationship or anything distract my greater love for you.

November

Thanksgiving and Praise

1

It is a good thing to give thanks unto the LORD, and to sing praises unto thy name, O most high: To shew forth thy lovingkindness in the morning, and thy faithfulness every night. (Ps 92:1, 2)

Start your day with praising Almighty God, and end it with gratitude for all his support.

2

I will mention the lovingkindnesses of the LORD, and the praises of the LORD, according to all that the LORD hath bestowed on us…. (Isa 63:7)

God, I thank and glorify your holy name for all your goodness upon me.

3

Pray without ceasing. In every thing give thanks: for this is the will of God in Christ Jesus concerning you. (1 Thess 5:17, 18)

As many may be enjoying lunch at noon, remember to thank him who at this same time was crucified for us.

4

Whoso offereth praise glorifieth me: and to him that ordereth his conversation aright will I shew the salvation of God. (Ps 50:23)

Thank God always, at least for bringing you to the very moment of thanking him.

5

By him therefore let us offer the sacrifice of praise to God continually, that is, the fruit of our lips giving thanks to his name. (Heb 13:15)

My Lord Jesus, let my words and deeds ever glorify your greatness.

6

...ye should shew forth the praises of him who hath called you out of darkness into his marvellous light. (1 Pet 2:9)

I gratefully praise you, the Light of the world, for enlightening me.

7

But God be thanked, that ye were the servants of sin, but ye have obeyed from the heart that form of doctrine which was delivered you. Being then made free from sin, ye became the servants of righteousness. (Rom 6:17, 18)

Let us show our sincere appreciation for the Lord's sacrifice by living righteously.

8

And a voice came out of the throne, saying, Praise our God, all ye his servants, and ye that fear him, both small and great. (Rev 19:5)

The Omnipotent seeks our heartfelt gratitude as a response for his love sacrifice.

9

Sing unto the LORD, O ye saints of his, and give thanks at the remembrance of his holiness. For his anger endureth but a moment; in his favour is life: weeping may endure for a night, but joy cometh in the morning. (Ps 30:4, 5)

Render thanks to the beneficent Lord even in challenging times.

10

Let the people praise thee, O God; let all the people praise thee. Then shall the earth yield her increase; and God, even our own God, shall bless us. (Ps 67:5, 6)

Instead of complaining and focusing on the negatives, I thank you, God, for everything.

11

Give thanks unto the LORD, call upon his name, make known his deeds among the people. Sing unto him, sing psalms unto him, talk ye of all his wondrous works. (1 Chr 16:8, 9)

Let others hear your words of "thank God" if you must speak of your success granted by him.

12

I will praise the name of God with a song, and will magnify him with thanksgiving. This also shall please the LORD.... (Ps 69:30, 31)

I appreciate your work in my life, Lord; please don't leave me.

13

Unto thee, O God, do we give thanks, unto thee do we give thanks: for that thy name is near thy wondrous works declare. (Ps 75:1)

God, I find no way to return all that you do for me except to ever thank you.

14

And the four and twenty elders, which sat before God on their seats, fell upon their faces, and worshipped God, Saying, We give thee thanks, O Lord God Almighty, which art, and wast, and art to come; because thou hast taken to thee thy great power, and hast reigned. (Rev 11:16, 17)

Exalting the King of Kings is union with the heavenly beings.

15

Let us come before his presence with thanksgiving, and make a joyful noise unto him with psalms. (Ps 95:2)

Lord, I am grateful for your love, grace, mercy, protection, guidance, blessings, and help.

16

But thanks be to God, which giveth us the victory through our Lord Jesus Christ. (1 Cor 15:57)

Thank you, God, for making your victory my triumph and joy.

17

Sing praises to God, sing praises: sing praises unto our King, sing praises. For God is the King of all the earth: sing ye praises with understanding. (Ps 47:6, 7)

Let our minds and hearts utter sincere appreciation for God's love.

18

And God is able to make all grace abound toward you; that ye, always having all sufficiency in all things, may abound to every good work....Thanks be unto God for his unspeakable gift. (2 Cor 9:8, 15)

God, help me to express gratitude for your countless blessings through good deeds.

19

Praise ye the LORD. *O give thanks unto the* LORD; *for he is good: for his mercy endureth for ever. (Ps 106:1)*

Our compassionate Savior is worthy of all glorification in heaven and earth.

20

Giving thanks unto the Father, which hath made us meet to be partakers of the inheritance of the saints in light. (Col 1:12)

I praise your mercy, Lord, for leading me to your light.

21

Oh that men would praise the LORD *for his goodness, and for his wonderful works to the children of men! And let them sacrifice the sacrifices of thanksgiving, and declare his works with rejoicing. (Ps 107:21, 22)*

I cannot ever thank you enough, Lord; I praise your kindness.

22

And whatsoever ye do in word or deed, do all in the name of the Lord Jesus, giving thanks to God and the Father by him. (Col 3:17)

Let all speech and actions be Christlike, thus declaring gratitude toward him.

23

I will offer to thee the sacrifice of thanksgiving, and will call upon the name of the LORD. I will pay my vows unto the LORD now in the presence of all his people. (Ps 116:17, 18)

Oh God, help me to always remember your goodness and keep my promises.

24

Speaking to yourselves in psalms and hymns and spiritual songs, singing and making melody in your heart to the LORD; Giving thanks always for all things unto God and the Father in the name of our LORD Jesus Christ. (Eph 5:19, 20)

Joyful is a thankful person, whose gratitude toward God is a good example.

25

I will extol thee, my God, O king; and I will bless thy name for ever and ever. Every day will I bless thee; and I will praise thy name for ever and ever. (Ps 145:1, 2)

I must thank God for everything and in any condition; blessed be God whether he gives or takes.

26

I will sing unto the LORD as long as I live: I will sing praise to my God while I have my being. (Ps 104:33)

Throughout life, whether healthy or ill, rich or poor, happy or afflicted, thank God.

27

Surely the righteous shall give thanks unto thy name: the upright shall dwell in thy presence. (Ps 140:13)

Help me to glorify you unceasingly, my Lord, for I am forever indebted to your love.

28

By thee have I been holden up from the womb:
thou art he that took me out of my mother's
bowels: my praise shall be continually of thee.
(Ps 71:6)

If we owe our earthly lives to God, how much
more should we thank him for the eternal gifts!

29

My lips shall utter praise, when thou hast
taught me thy statutes. (Ps 119:171)

Lord, the holy life you teach me puts joy in my
heart and your praise on my lips.

30

Praise ye the LORD. Praise, O ye servants of the
LORD, praise the name of the LORD....From the
rising of the sun unto the going down of the
same the LORD's name is to be praised. (Ps
113:1, 3)

Glorify God every morning for his blessings,
and worship him before sleep for keeping you
as his own.

December

Happiness

1

Yet I will rejoice in the LORD, I will joy in the God of my salvation. (Hab 3:18)

I will rejoice in God, my helper, when I off-load all anxiety, fear, and troubles onto him.

2

...this day is holy unto our LORD: neither be ye sorry; for the joy of the LORD is your strength....Hold your peace, for the day is holy; neither be ye grieved. (Neh 8:10, 11)

Lord, support me on the path of holiness and gladden my heart always.

3

Let the righteous be glad; let them rejoice before God: yea, let them exceedingly rejoice. (Ps 68:3)

The saints rightfully rejoice because God has crowns and unimaginable rewards for them.

4

Jesus spake unto them, saying, Be of good cheer; it is I; be not afraid. (Matt 14:27)

Lord, make me come to you treading all fear by the joy you provide.

5

Behold, this is the joy of his way....Till he fill thy mouth with laughing, and thy lips with rejoicing. (Job 8:19, 21)

The Sovereign Lord gently sustains us and ensures our happiness by his providence.

6

Rejoice in the LORD always: and again I say, Rejoice. (Phil 4:4)

Lord, I want the true joy by abiding in you, not through worldly matters.

7

Happy is that people, that is in such a case: yea, happy is that people, whose God is the Lord. *(Ps 144:15)*

God, give me inner joy to cheer everyone around, as was the case with early Christians whose happiness spread to nonbelievers.

8

Be of good cheer: for I believe God, that it shall be even as it was told me. (Act 27:25)

Being with our Shepherd, we lack nothing and seek nobody to fill our hearts with true happiness.

9

His lord said unto him, "Well done, thou good and faithful servant...enter thou into the joy of thy lord." (Matt 25:21)

Lord, help me be faithful to your ways that I may hear this expression at the end of my life.

10

Thy words were found, and I did eat them; and thy word was unto me the joy and rejoicing of mine heart: for I am called by thy name, O LORD *God of hosts. (Jer 15:16)*

God, the more I read your words of spirit and life, the more joy I feel.

11

These things have I spoken unto you, that my joy might remain in you, and that your joy might be full. (John 15:11)

We experience unwavering happiness when we practice God's teachings.

12

I will greatly rejoice in the LORD, *my soul shall be joyful in my God; for he hath clothed me with the garments of salvation, he hath covered me with the robe of righteousness.... (Isa 61:10)*

Lord, guide us to your eternal kingdom, where we rejoice in victory and salvation.

13

But the fruit of the Spirit is love, joy, peace, longsuffering, gentleness, goodness, faith, meekness, temperance.... (Gal 5:22, 23)

God wants us always to be happy and bear good fruits leading to eternal bliss.

14

Surely he hath borne our griefs, and carried our sorrows: yet we did esteem him stricken, smitten of God, and afflicted. (Isa 53:4)

Lord, let nothing depress me as you bore all our sadness.

15

My brethren, count it all joy when ye fall into divers temptations; Knowing this, that the trying of your faith worketh patience. (Jas 1:2, 3)

Rejoicing in problems? Yes, because we become purified as we implore God's rescue, then see his work.

16

Because thou hast been my help, therefore in the shadow of thy wings will I rejoice. (Ps 63:7)

Oh Savior, gladden us with your immediate solutions for our increasing problems.

17

But rejoice, inasmuch as ye are partakers of Christ's sufferings; that, when his glory shall be revealed, ye may be glad also with exceeding joy. (1 Pet 4:13)

All suffering for Christ's sake leads to splendor and elation.

18

Serve the LORD with gladness: come before his presence with singing. (Ps 100:2)

Let us rejoice in worshiping God and forsaking sinful pleasures.

19

For his anger endureth but a moment; in his favour is life: weeping may endure for a night, but joy cometh in the morning. (Ps 30:5)

Lord, make my day begin and end in happiness for your goodness encompasses my life.

20

...he that keepeth the law, happy is he. (Prov 29:18)

Living by God's laws, I rejoice in his righteousness; obeying the laws of the land, I remain happy and free.

21

Make me to hear joy and gladness; that the bones which thou hast broken may rejoice. (Ps 51:8)

God, make me joyful in sanctity after you correct me with your gentleness.

22

Ye now therefore have sorrow: but I will see you again, and your heart shall rejoice, and your joy no man taketh from you. (John 16:22)

In the afterlife, God obliterates all sadness and the bitter memory of sin.

23

How long shall I...sorrow in my heart daily?... But I have trusted in thy mercy; my heart shall rejoice in thy salvation. (Ps 13:2, 5)

As sure is God's mercy, so will be our happiness.

24

Behold, we count them happy which endure. Ye have heard of the patience of Job, and have seen the end of the Lord; that the Lord is very pitiful, and of tender mercy. (Jas 5:11)

Contentment comes when we benefit from character-building experiences permitted by God.

25

Be glad then, ye children of Zion, and rejoice in the LORD your God.... (Joel 2:23)

Lord, I want to be among your people, exulting as they enter heaven with many virtues.

26

Blessed are ye, when men shall revile you, and persecute you, and shall say all manner of evil against you falsely, for my sake. Rejoice, and be exceeding glad: for great is your reward in heaven.... (Matt 5:11, 12)

Support me to joyfully accept all persecutions for bearing your holy name, my Lord.

27

As sorrowful, yet alway rejoicing; as poor, yet making many rich; as having nothing, and yet possessing all things. (2 Cor 6:10)

God, make me focus on the delight of heavenly treasures, not materialism.

28

Thou wilt shew me the path of life: in thy presence is fulness of joy; at thy right hand there are pleasures for evermore. (Ps 16:11)

With eternal rewards the Lord gladdens his faithful who persist on his holy ways.

29

For the kingdom of God is not meat and drink; but righteousness, and peace, and joy in the Holy Spirit. (Rom 14:17)

Lord, make me experience your kingdom now and forever.

30

The ransomed of the LORD shall return, and come to Zion with songs and everlasting joy upon their heads: they shall obtain joy and gladness, and sorrow and sighing shall flee away. (Isa 35:10)

God, let all our sacrifices and tribulations be consumed by your perpetual jubilation.

Whom having not seen, ye love; in whom, though now ye see him not, yet believing, ye rejoice with joy unspeakable and full of glory: receiving the end of your faith, even the salvation of your souls. (1 Pet 1:8, 9)

My Lord, as I began in your faith, so help me reach your kingdom while I joyfully abide in your love.